CONTENTS

Introduction
The Mindset Behind Our Money   1
Common Money Mistakes   6
Establishing Good Money Behaviors   16
Investing in the Stock Market   22
What It All Comes Down To   27

INTRODUCTION

Money: we can't live with it, we can't live without it. Everything in our lives seems to revolve around money. Food, shelter, transportation, utilities: all these things are provided to us. All we need to do is fork over some of that cold hard cash. Money is universal, coming in different forms from across the world. However, with that need comes scarcity. Class systems emerge, economies change; all these things influence the amount of money in our wallets at any given time.

Living in America, one of the most affluent countries in the world, you would expect many people to be in a better place financially than they would be in other countries in the world. America is leading the world with the highest gross domestic product (GDP), currently reaching 20.49 trillion. We are one of the global powerhouses when it comes to trading and commerce, and our economy has benefited from it. Although our money troubles are less severe than those of the people living in struggling countries, recent surveys suggest that 7 out of 10 American claim to experience a lack of financial stability. According to Forbes, only about 30% of American consider themselves to be financially healthy, with the majority only being able to get by. The sad fact is that many people, including those above the poverty line, are spending more than they are earning. Urban Institute recently conducted a survey shining a light onto how bad things have gotten for some people. They state that 4 out of 10 American struggle with pay for their basic needs. These include things like housing, utilities, and groceries. Despite the success of our economy at large, those at the bottom are still struggling to pay for many of the costs that come with living.

Perhaps this can partly be blamed on the status quo. Class structure within American society is a concept that has been debated for years. Many people insist that the class status is a myth; that the place a person is born financially into doesn't impact their future financial status. They use the argument that many millionaires are self-made, starting from the bottom and working their way up. This is true that the problem doesn't necessarily hinge on the class a person was born into. It's always a possibility a person will start a business from the ground up and break through the status quo. However, the lack of opportunities a person on the bottom has to gain the success of someone from a higher class is where things start to get messy. It's very difficult for people on the lower class stratifications to get enough money to graduate from college or even enter a trade school, aspects of life that would be invaluable if you wanted to get a good job or start your own business.

With so many high paying jobs having a degree requirement, the idea of reaching those goals seems like wishful thinking to some people. In fact, in some ways it might benefit the American economy as a whole if certain people are kept where they are. Essential workers are the backbone of any society. Without people like construction workers, farmers, and health care workers, our flourishing society would crumble under its own weight. These jobs are more often than not tended to by people of the working class. Rather than paying for college tuition (which is oftentimes more expensive than even the middle class can afford) they opt to study trades that will prepare them for manual labor jobs and industry work. Without the working class, these jobs would have very few people capable of filling them. If no one were to take these jobs, it could bring irreparable damage to our current way of life.

Sound's cruel, doesn't it? The poor stay poor and the rich stay rich; it completely goes against what America preaches. The "American Dream" apparently only applies to some members of society. For that reason, it's easy for people who are less fortunate to blame those at the top for their hardships.

We've all heard the phrase, "money is the root of all evil." Originally taken from Christian mythos, the phrase has become synonymous with decadence, class stratification, and corporate greed. One of the most common misquotes that people still use today, people often use the inherent evil of money to explain why we have many of the problems we have today. However, money itself isn't necessarily the problem. At the end of the day, the only value on things like paper money, gold, and diamonds is purely based on the societal significance we place on them. The original quote from 1 Timothy 6:10 is as follows: "For the love of money is the root of all evil: which while some coveted after, they have erred from the faith, and pierced themselves through with many sorrows." "Love of money"; love being the operative word.

Money gives people a modicum of power, what we do with that power is up to the person themselves. Money can be used to build hospitals, donate to charities, and fund non-profit groups that help the environment. As stated by Bradley Vinson, an author that focuses on financial self-help books, "Money is a tool. Used properly it makes something beautiful; used wrong, it makes a mess!" People who are more likely to use money for their own devices is where the whole concept gets a bit messy.

But do we really love money? Or do we love what money can provide? Money is a transitory thing, a step towards receiving what we genuinely want. It's the same as receiving a ticket for the Metro, or a VIP access card for a concert. Those things only have power because they give access to the amenities and luxuries that we wouldn't be able to experience otherwise. Ironically, the transitory nature of our money is what ultimately causes many people to devalue it. The act of saving money has become an undesirable task for many people. According to the Federal Reserve, the majority of American only have about 1000 to 5000 dollars in their savings account at any given time. They also stated that "Thirty-one percent of non-retired respondents reported having no retirement savings or pension, including 19% of those ages 55 to 64." There is so much we could be using that money for, yet we let it sit there like stagnant water. The urge to spend our hard-earned money rather than save it for a later day is one of the effects of us devaluing the worth of our own money.

When we become obsessed with the power money can give us, it doesn't just damage the monetary side of our lives. It also has the ability to creep into parts of our lives that we wouldn't expect. Constantly coveting that crisp dollar bill can have adverse effects on your relationships with other people. You might be hesitant to pay back a friend who lent you money, you might feel the need to avoid going to social gatherings to avoid splitting the bill, and it might spark relationship trouble between you and your significant other. Yes, money can affect your marriage, and it's one of the major contributors to the divorce rate. According to a survey done by TD Bank, 40% of divorcees claim that they've had frequent fights with their spouse over money related issues and concerns. Many couples find themselves refusing to talk to each other about finances because of how heated the arguments can get. This is counterintuitive, as it often causes more arguments in the future when two people aren't able to read each other's minds on what they should be spending on. When money is put first, people are often put second, and our close relationships can suffer for it.

There's also the amount of stress that our finances can ultimately put on our minds and bodies. Financial stress is often a side effect of poor financial planning. According to a Money-Rates survey, 35% of the people they interviewed stated that their biggest concerns in terms of finances were how they were going to afford rent, mortgage, and credit card payments. These people are often concerned with trying to survive paycheck to paycheck, with very little money left after their expenses are paid. This lack of leeway can put a lot of stress on a person. According to Cambridge Credit Counseling Corp., "The stress of having too much credit card debt, college loan payments, or medical bills can weigh on a person and cause severe anxiety and depression." In addition, financial stress can cause a variety of physical ailments as well. These include, but are not limited to, weight gain/loss, gastrointestinal problems, insomnia, high blood pressure, and even substance abuse.

So now that we're all well aware of the effects that a poor money mindset can have on you, we're once again brought to the question of what can we do about it? In the end, it all comes down to how we conduct ourselves. This may be a bitter pill for us to swallow. After all, it's naturally easier for us to blame money as a concept or the society we live in than it is for us to blame ourselves. However, this can also give us a little hope that our financial situation doesn't have to be permanent. While it's true that some people have an easier time accumulating income, in reality almost everyone has the capacity to manage and save their money responsibly. It just takes more time and effort on our part to do so. The first step is changing our mindset. As Jaspreet Singh, entrepreneur and content creator for Minority Mindset stated, "Think from the mindset of the consumer and be the provider." When we focus on building wealth through strategy and awareness, rather than feeling bad for ourselves, then we'll have an easier time accruing wealth than the majority of society.

THE MINDSET BEHIND OUR MONEY

Before we analyze what we can do to fix our money troubles, it's important for us to figure out what is the root problem behind us. I'm not talking about wage or class differences; the main problem is something that is mostly within our control. More often than not, the root problem of our money troubles is ourselves. This doesn't necessarily mean that we're not working hard enough or we don't have a good enough jobs. It can simply be a matter of psychology.

Realizing how we think about money can make all the difference to our current circumstances. Have you ever thought about how you spend? What would you think if you were gifted a wad of cash? What is your first impulse when you receive your paycheck? Your answers to these questions could determine the way you perceive money as a concept. Your view on money is something you want to keep in mind in order to decode where your root problem is regarding your finances.

According to BBC Teach, there are four ways people typically view money: money as power, money as generosity, money as security, and money as freedom. These outlooks shape how we spend, how we save, and how we give money.

Money As Power

While it's an unfortunate truth that money makes the world go round, those who see money as power have a far more exaggerated view of that statement. There is an old saying that goes back to the deepest reaches of past human civilization: "He who has the gold makes the rules." People who view money as power treat that statement as gospel. To them, money is both a show of dominance and a status symbol. An abundance of it can get to people's heads, making them think they have the world at their fingertips.

People who see money as power are more likely to buy expensive things juts to impress people. Expenses such as designer brands, luxury cars, and newest technology often come with the connotation that they are designed for the elite of society. For that reason, it's socially stylish for us to wear the latest from *Dolce and Gibbana*, then it is to wear something you bought at the clearance aisle.

This mindset doesn't just apply to the wealthy elite, people with very little money can have this mindset as well. Why do you think get-rich-quick schemes are so prominent in modern day society? People on the lower end of the financial spectrum also want a taste of the power money can give. That lust for money and the status and power it provides can blind a person to poor investments and bad spending habits, ultimately causing them to lose the money they so crave.

Money As Generosity

Those who view money as generosity may see their recent raise as a way to treat their friends and family to something special.

These people may feel responsible for other people's health and wellbeing, such as having to take care of a child or an aging parent. As a result, they'll be more likely to put those people's needs and desires before their own. While this might be an innocent enough mindset on its own, these types of people often neglect their own needs and think very little about their own financial situation. They may opt to treat their friends and families or donate to charities, rather than saving up for their own financial emergencies.

To add insult to injury, these kinds of people may even feel guilty when they're given money to use on themselves. They may feel unworthy of their own good fortune, or that they could use it to make someone else happy. For some, seeing a large number in their bank account is damaging to their psyche. This financial martyr complex can prevent them from saving up or even being able to enjoy their own wealth. It's important for people to make their own financial situation a priority, even if they have other things in their lives that they're responsible for.

Money As Security

People who view money as security are more likely to save their money. They may search for more cost-efficient options at the store, regularly deposit funds into their savings account, and constantly be on the lookout for way of accruing positive interest.

One might thing that this is a perfect mindset to have with money, however even this mentality has its detriments. Being too frugal can negatively decrease your quality of life. When you are only concerned with saving money, you can't allow yourself to enjoy your good fortune. According to surveys, 12% of people stated that they regretted being so cheap with themselves and refusing to allow themselves to enjoy the money that they had.
This overly frugal mindset can even be disadvantageous to you financially. Being too focused on security can also make you hesi-

tant to take risks, such as investing in stocks and bonds. The stock market is a great way to earn money on the side, but there is always the possibility that you'll end up losing money rather than earning it. That lack of security turns many people off, which can actually end up costing them money. It's important to remember that nothing good comes without some form of risk. If the fear of losing is making you turn down good opportunities, then that inaction will only hurt you in the long run.

Money As Freedom

People who view money as freedom are more likely to value experiences over money. They're free spirits, not wanted to be tied down by a plan or responsibilities. Life is short, and they want to experience all of it in the small amount of time they have on earth. This mindset is commonly associated with young people who are just starting out, as they have very few responsibilities at the time other than to take care of themselves. They may see money as a means of gaining their independence, such as being able to move to a new house or being able to travel across the world. To them, money is a transition: a step towards what they truly want.

For this reason, these kinds of people often neglect to save or invest their money. This will ultimately be detrimental for them, as they may find themselves at a loss of what to do when faced with a financial emergency. While it's important to be able to savor the good fortune you have, it's equally—if not more—important for you to save money for whatever misfortune inevitably comes your way.

Money Disorders

For some people, their money troubles don't simply stem from a certain mindset, but from an actual mental disorder. Many people might not realize that money disorders are an actual thing, let alone how common they are in modern society. The biggest connection we can make is that it shares similarities with eating disorders, where eating (or lack thereof) is used to satisfy a certain psychological desire. Brad Klonz, psychologist and associate professor at Creighton University, defines money disorders thusly: "In general, a money disorder is a chronic pattern of self-defeating or self-destructive financial behaviors."

Among these disorders are gambling addictions, compulsive spending, compulsive hoarding, financial infidelity, etc. Like many addictions, these are caused by mental processes in the brain rewarding years of bad habits. These patterns of behavior can make budgeting, financial planning, and developing positive financial behaviors way more difficult. Even as you make good financial choices, you're always going to be fighting against the urge to indulge in your disorder. It's not just a matter of changing your mindset, but also changing your brain chemistry as well. It's important that people with these problems get help before they even begin to fix their financial situation.

While we can't change the external factors that may have an effect on our money—such as economic recessions, position on the poverty line, or accessibility to higher education—there is one thing that we can affect: our own personal money mindset. How we choose to view the necessary evil that is money can make all the difference. Once we adjust our mindset, we'll be able to make the necessary changes in our lives to find solutions to our financial situation and get ourselves to where we want to be in life. It doesn't matter who you are, what background you have, or what mental disabilities you may have developed over the years; everyone has the power to better themselves financially.

COMMON MONEY MISTAKES

Now that we're aware of the mindsets we have ingrained in our minds that may affect how we treat our money, we should turn our attention to the behaviors we exhibit in our daily lives. There are many things we do with our money that have a bigger impact on us than we realize. The worst part is, we don't even realize the little things we do are costing us so much money. Every choice we make when we make a run to the grocery store, go shopping with friends, or go browsing the internet not only has an effect on the amount of money we have in our wallets, but cements habits that will affect the money we'll have in the future. During this segment, we'll go through the most common money mistakes that people make and analyzing the full effect they have on us.

Frivolous Spending

One of the most common money mistakes the populace at large makes is engaging in frivolous spending habits. These include actions like overspending, impulse buying, and engaging to often in retail therapy. We've all been there: you suddenly see something in the store that you just have to have or you're browsing online and stumble across an item that is just calling out your name. Impulse buying gives provides us a surge of dopamine, giving us a "buyer's high". However, this habit is often followed by "buyer's remorse" when you take another look at your receipt and realize just how much you spent. This not only has the effect of lessening your finances, but it also has the capacity to make you dependent on shopping to feel better. This results in a vicious cycle of feeling bad, engaging in retail therapy, and then feeling bad about wasting money.

When it comes to compulsive spending these feelings are only compounded. Statistically, 6% of the US population fits the criteria of being a compulsive spender. According to clinical psychiatrist Scott Bea, "Compulsive shoppers have frequent buying episodes or overpowering urges to purchase items. This behavior is linked to feelings of worthlessness in addition to a lack of power." This addiction has been likened to gambling or sex addiction, as the sensations that come with the act of spending often bring the person more rewards than the objects themselves.

The innovation of online shopping hasn't made dealing with these unwanted desires any easier, as makes it even easier for people to satiate and indulge in that high. When buying something is as simple as clicking a button, we often find ourselves overcome with that "buyer's high" sensation when we realize we can purchase anything from anywhere and receive it in the comfort of our own home. This often causes people to lose track of how much they're spending. Adding with that the cost of shipping prices, and some people may find themselves spending $300 dollars in one sitting and not even notice it. This kind of behavior is a slippery slope for anyone, not just those with the compulsive spending habit, and if not reigned in it can have damaging effects to your financial situation.

Excessive Recurring Payments

You know that Netflix account you have? That subscription to People magazine? The money that leaves your account every time rent is due? All of those aspects of your life are classified under recurring payments. Recurring payment is a payment medium where the consumer gives a provider permission to pull funds out of their account at certain intervals in exchange for services.

There are two types of recurring payments: regular/fixed payments and irregular/varied payments. As stated by Subscriptions, "With fixed or regular payments, the customers are charged the same amount each time. [...] With variable or irregular recurring payments, the amount charged is subject to change based on the customers' usage of the product or service. These are common payment methods that you'd be charged for utilities, online streaming services and magazine subscriptions. Recurring payments were made to be a convenient alternative; it frees the consumer from having to worry about late fees or constantly having to insert their billing information when the month is up.

While it may seem convenient to rely on auto-pay, the fact that they don't require any attention on your part comes at the risk of you losing track of the amount of money you're spending. This makes it more difficult for you to budget around them. There is also the problem of accruing too many of these subscriptions and subsequently losing track of them. It's easy for people to forget that they have a monthly subscription to *Cosmopolitan* when they haven't read a single issue in about two years. Having too many subscriptions that you don't need or even use that often means you're opening yourself up to the prospect of unnecessary spending. It's important for you to keep track of all the services that include recurring payments. That way you can analyze all the money you're spending monthly and get rid of subscriptions that you don't use or could do without.

Accruing Excess Debt

When dealing with finances, it's not possible to take every probable outcome into account. Sometimes things come up in life. Sometimes there's an emergency that needs to be tended to immediately and you simply don't have the funds to cover it. You might look towards taking out a loan, put it on credit, or even ask a friend or family member to help you pay it off. Sometimes it's necessary to spend money you don't have at the moment. However, it's important for the act of borrowing money to not become a pattern of behavior. Accruing too much debt can be a precarious financial situation to be in.

Debt is a problem that our society is well aware of: according to Debt.org, American is in the middle of a consumer debt crisis, with the total recorded debt being around $14.9 trillion. Mortgages, student loans, and credit card payments are just a few of the debts many Americans have to stress about. For that reason, many people find themselves overextended. Overextension occurs when a person has more debt than they are able to repay. According to Investopedia, "consumers who must use more than a third of their net income to repay debt are generally considered to be overextended." This can place a lot of financial stress on a person as they scramble to pay off their debts. Some people may even choose to borrow more money or take out more credit so they can pay off the money that they previously borrowed. This is a precarious action to take as it can cause a snowball effect, causing the individual to build more and more debt as time goes on. Essentially, you are using debt to pay more debt. This action also has the capacity to ruin your credit score, negatively impacting what loans you may receive in the future, which could mean you could eventually reach the end of the road and be unable to take out any more loans to pay off existing loans. Or worse, you could risk being unable to use those loans for a financial emergency.

Paying Debt With Savings

This brings us to another common problem that people have with their finances. When we find ourselves in debt, we begin to feel like we have a weight pressing down on us. There's always that dark cloud looming over us, reminding us with every payment that we make that there's still money that we owe. Being in a stressful situation, many people are tempted to tap into their hard-earned savings to pay off these debts. While this may seem like a no-brainer—after all, that's what savings are for, right?—using your savings to pay off debts is actually detrimental to you in the long-run.

Depleting your savings like this simply puts you at more risk of accruing more debt in the future. Savings are meant to be an emergency fund, used to pay for essentials that you need in the moment. Right now, while you may be all too aware of the money you owe, you still have time to pay those off in the future. If you end up using your savings to pay off debts that don't need your immediate attention, then you run the risk of not being able to pay for hospital bills or paying for car repairs.

If you truly need to pay off debt, it's important to structure your payments on triage. Toxic debt (debt with an interest of more than 15%) should be your first priority when paying it off, as the amount can increase rapidly in a short amount of time. After those are paid off, you should instead focus on your adding money to your savings account and keeping it there.

Living Paycheck To Paycheck

For many people, the act of accumulating income is a slow and labored process, as they tirelessly work towards constantly paying their bills on time. The term "living paycheck to paycheck" refers to when a person solely relies on their employment to pay for their costs of living. The entirety of their salaries more often than not go towards expenses like rent, utilities and groceries. As a result, these people have very little breathing room in terms of money, meaning they have little to no savings in their account.

The concept of living paycheck to paycheck is normally a characteristic associated with the working/working poor class. However, as the years pass, it's becoming a rising trend even among households that are classified as middle class. According to NPR, "a third of U.S. adults say they are having difficulty covering everyday costs such as food, rent or car payments." It seems everyone from single parents, young upstarts, and unfortunately even some members of the senior community are susceptible to this draining way of living.

This kind of lifestyle puts a person in a lot of financial risk, as if they were to find themselves in a position of unemployment it would put them in a dangerous financial situation. It also puts them at risk of not being able to pay for an emergency situation should the need arise. This may be a difficult problem to fix because the person's current situation leaves very little leeway for them to make changes to their finances. They find themselves stuck in this rut; only being able to get by with no hope of climbing out again. It's still possible for someone in this situation to accumulate savings, but it's going to take a substantial amount of time, effort and planning to do so. It may seem counterintuitive, but your main focus should be to put as much money as you can afford into your savings account. This might make things a little tighter expense-wise, but it will only help you in the long run when you need that money for an emergency.

Abusing Home Equity

Homeowners are privy to a lot of perks that renters could never dream of. The freedom of having your own space, having more control over the housing costs, and being able to fully customize your home are some of the benefits of having a house of your own. However, one thing homeowners don't realize is the fact that your home can actually accrue money.

According to Investopedia, "Home equity is the portion of a home's current value that the owner actually possesses at any given time." This is influenced by the amount of the mortgage paid off, the size of the down payment initially paid, and the home's value within the homeowner's market. Having good home equity can be invaluable to the current homeowner, as it can actually be used as a form of credit. Home equity line of credit (or HELOC) can be used to obtain lower rates from lenders and even borrow money from the value of your house. However, at the end of the day, debt is still debt. It may be tempting to use your home as a credit card to pay for the things you want, but making a habit of it could hurt you rather than help you.

Although the interest rates on HELOC are lower than what you would see on a credit card, those numbers still add up. There's also the fact that home equity is subject to change. According to Forbes, "Appreciation is independent of your equity position. Appreciation depends on market forces like migration patterns, area wage growth and remaining land availability." This means that within a year, your house's value could drastically change, thus affecting the amount of equity a person has. So it's important that you don't end up abusing your home equity for things that aren't entirely necessary.

The best things you can use home equity for are emergency expenses, consolidations, and investments; so if you're thinking of buying a new car or going on vacation, it's best to save up rather than abuse your home equity.

Gambling

It's important for our quality of life to be able to enjoy our money. It doesn't do us as people any favors if we hoard our every paycheck and put all our money into savings. Sometimes the best thing you can do with your money is enjoy it. However, how we enjoy it can make all the difference. Certain pastimes foster certain mindsets that can be detrimental to how you handle money in the future, and gambling is no exception.

Gambling is one of the worst things you can do with your money. The allure of easy wealth may be hard to ignore, but it's important to remember the statistics. The stats are always weighted towards the casino, slot machines having a one in about 34 million chance of the person winning, according to Investopedia. These statistics don't simply refer to the slot machines you would see in Vegas; it also refers to lottery tickets, card games, and online gambling.

Most people have the good sense to realize that this isn't a smart way to earn money and it shouldn't be something we rely on financially. However, that hasn't stopped the majority of people from trying their luck. Statistics show that 80% of American adults gamble annually, and moreover, 3 out of 5 gamblers are addicts.

So why exactly do we do it? The answer lies in our psychology. The reason gambling is so addictive has to do with its ability to tap into our body's "reward system." The thrill of gambling releases the neurotransmitter dopamine into the brain, giving us a sensation similar to what we would feel when we succeed in our goals or receive a well-earned compliment. The druglike effect of betting money we could easily lose is what causes many people to develop an addiction to it.

This could complicate our plans to become more financially secure. In essence, it's like an alcoholic trying to quit drinking while also working part time as a bartender. We're around money every day, and the urge to gamble can rise with every paycheck. The best thing you can do is go cold turkey, avoiding gambling at all costs in order to make a dent in your finances. If you have or suspect that you have a gambling addiction, it's vital that you seek help before you attempt to better your financial situation.

Avoiding The Stock Market

The stock market has been around for centuries, with the earliest versions recorded in the 1500s. It's a place where people buy stocks and shares off of companies in exchange for a percentage of their earned wealth. However, despite its long-standing presence in our society, the act of investing has become far less common with current generations.

The threat of putting your money into something without knowing whether you'll end up earning or losing is something the later generations are hesitant to do. According to Gallup, only 37% of young American have invested in the stock market. This most likely due to the stock market crash of 2008, where stockholders lost trillions of dollars in a short span of time. Since then, many young Americans have opted instead towards saving their money, rather than investing and running the risk of losing it.

While this on the surface might seem like a good choice, this may end up costing you money in the long run. While it's a good idea to put money into your savings, you're likely to get far more from investing. Savings accounts are made for you to keep your money in for long stretches of time; this means that the amount of money you earn will be far more if you continue saving for decades, rather than taking that money out within the year. Investing isn't meant for you to hoard money in for years; it's a process in which you give companies your money in return for stocks. On average, investing can accrue 25% more money than a savings account, allowing you to earn more money in a shorter amount of time. By making the choice not to invest, you are actually shooting yourself in the foot financially, missing out on a lot of money that you could have been earning.

It's amazing the impact the little things we do in our life have when we take a closer took at them. Some people might consider themselves very financially sound, not even realizing the everyday habits they indulge in (or don't indulge in) that are causing them to lose money. However, that's the purpose of this exercise: to identify and address the negative behaviors we participate in to make the appropriate changes. The first step to achieving change is always to address that you have a problem. These are habits that apply to everyone. A person of the upper class can have the same bad tendencies as a person of the working class. And that means that no matter who you are, where you stand in the class system, or what background you come from— everyone has the power to change their bad money habits and better their financial situation.

ESTABLISHING GOOD MONEY BEHAVIORS

Now that we know what not to do, it's important for us to figure out what steps we can take to better our financial situation. Depending on your financial situation, this could be a difficult task to complete. Once we realize the bad habits we participate in during our everyday lives, it's easy for us to realize what we're doing wrong and correct it. However, the act of creating new positive behaviors with money can be a long and arduous task. It's also important for you to figure out a plan that best suits your financial situation. The amount of breathing room a person has with their money if they're a middle-class professional is very different from that of a working-class single parent.

In order to figure out what plan is best for you, it's important to analyze your current situation thoroughly and figure out what you can and can't afford to change. Your first step to bettering your financial situation is to create a financial plan. This might come as a no-brainer, and you might have a barebones financial plan already in place. Budgeting is in itself a financial plan; a method in which we use to divide up our money to pay our expenses.

However, budgeting only helps you to get by, not increase your finances. It's important that we also make changes to how we spend in order to increase the amount of money we have left over. This involves cutting expenses, putting some money aside in savings, and creating financial goals. When creating a financial plan, it's important to look for every avenue in which you can save money.

Cutting Expenses

Our first option to do so would be to cut our expenses. The phrase "cutting expenses" often has a bit of a stigma attached to it. To many people it means living on a shoe-string budget, depriving them from many of the things that they enjoy in life. People are quick to go towards the extremes, such as going without dinner for a week or going without the internet for a while. However, cutting expenses doesn't necessarily have to mean refusing to buy certain things; it can simply be a matter of finding more cost-efficient options.

One way you can do this is by cutting down on fast food. It might be tempting to head to Wendy's or McDonalds to get a bite to eat before work, but making a habit of it will cause those numbers to add up. If you really have to eat something while you're on the road, try stepping into the convenience store for a quick snack to tide you over. A lot of the options there are less expensive than what you would see at fast food places. Getting a hotdog and a drink separately can take a huge chunk out of your expenditures.

Another easy way that you can cut your expenses is by avoiding buying name brand items. Most people don't realize how expensive name brands are compared to their generic brand alternatives. At the end of the day a name brand bottle of Advil does the same as the store brand pain reliever drug. While the name on the bottle may be nothing to write home about, they're far more cost-efficient than constantly buying their more famous alternatives.

It's also important when you're working towards cutting your expenses to take into account recurring payments. Your money might be slowly leaking from the amount of paid subscriptions you own. It's important to identify what you can and cannot live without to reduce the amount of money you're spending on needless things. By sticking to these positive habits, you'll find yourself with more money to work with.
It would also help if you were to be covered by insurance. I know; getting insurance for things like health care seems like wishful thinking for some people. However, if your employer doesn't provide insurance, you may be eligible to apply for private health insurance. Although it's important to have an emergency fund set aside for when you need it, insurance can be a lifesaver when it comes to having to pay for emergency expenses.

Add To Your Savings Account

Once you have more money to work with, it might be tempting for you to go out and treat yourself. But before you even think about doing so, it's important that you set aside some money on the side. One of the most important things you can do is start adding to your savings account. It's important to remember the amount of time your money is in your savings account also has an impact on it.

When you place money into your savings account, over time it will begin to build interest. The longer your savings are in your account, the more interest it will accrue. As a rule of thumb, most experts say that you should strive to put 20% of your income into your savings account each month. While this may seem like a lot, this will only benefit you in the long-run. Let's say that you put $100 into your savings account. The average simple interest rate for savings accounts is around 6%. This means that by the end of the year, you'll have 106 dollars in your account. That may not seem like much, but if the money is consistently added to the savings account, then the interest will only be further compounded. Let's say you have $5000 dollars in your savings account; if that money continues to accrue interest, then by the end of the year you'll have $5300 total in your account. However, it's important to remember that some savings accounts have interest rates higher or lower than 6%, meaning there's the possibility of gaining more (or less) money over time.

It's also important to decide ahead of time what you intend to use your savings for. Some people use savings as an emergency fund, while others put money into their account so they can make a down payment later on in life. Deciding what you want to do with that money in the future is important because some savings accounts will penalize you for taking out money too soon. It's important to do your research, as well as read up on hidden fees that might be involved in choosing a certain savings account.

Set Financial Goals

Now that you have more money to work with, it's important to figure out what you want to do with it. I'm not talking about going on a spending spree or treating you and your friends to a night out. This is about investing in your future. Setting financial goals is a good way for you to plan your spending in ways that will benefit you in the long run.

According to Investopedia, there are three types of financial goals: short-term, mid-term, and long-term. Short-term financial goals are these easiest to fulfill, and include but are not limited to paying off credit cards, creating a budget, or establishing an emergency fund. They can be fulfilled in a short amount of time; some of which will probably only take a month to complete. Completing these small goals will help you to work up to the larger ones.

Mid-term goals require a little more work. It's important to remember that you should focus on your mid-term goals after the short-term goals have been tended to, as the short-term goals require your immediate attention. Actions that fall into the category of mid-term goals include saving up for insurance or paying off student loans. These will take considerably more time to complete, lasting for months or even years before you reach the end result.

Long-term goals are the ones people are most familiar with. Actions such as establishing a 401k or saving to get your children through college are huge investments that will take years, possibly decades of time saving up for. For that reason, many people are so intimidated by them that they neglect to put any money into those financial goals. That is one of the worst mistakes a person can make. By developing a self-defeating attitude towards retirement or college, it ensures that you'll never reach those goals. The best thing you can do is save a little at a time, slowly chipping away at the impending expenses, until the end result is far smaller than they would have been if you never started saving.

Once you create financial goals, that doesn't mean that you're locked into it. In fact, experts encourage people to make adjustments to your goals as time goes on. In the words of Investopedia: "Annual financial planning gives you an opportunity to formally review your goals, update them, and review your progress since last year." Within a short span of time your financial situation can change, so it's important for you to adjust your goals to suit your financial needs.

Change Your Money Mindset

This was touched upon in the previous segments, but there is a substantial connection the mind has with money. Believe it or not how we view money can make all the difference in how we handle our finances. According to More Than Your Money, Inc., "There are two common attitudes toward money, one of optimism and abundance and one of scarcity and pessimism." It's pretty straightforward: more money means the person is more optimistic about their situation, less money means the person will be more pessimistic about their situation. However, neither of these situations are necessarily a good thing.

If a person is given an abundance of money in a short period of time, their first thought might be to spend it. New house, new car, designer clothes; the works. The abundance of money leaves the person feeling overconfident, not having enough knowledge of how to spend it. This is the reason many previously successful celebrities end up filing for bankruptcy.

Conversely, if a person is experiencing a scarcity in their finances, they may allow their pessimism to take over. Many people in this category may have a poor relationship with money; they may come from a family that was never financially stable or they may simply view money in a negative light. By having the mindset of simply taking what they can get, they may be unwilling to take risks or feel as though they can't afford to put any money into their savings.

When we're viewing our financial situation, it's important to be a realist; seeing our situation for what it is. Maybe things aren't entirely okay. Maybe you're going through some financial straits and don't know how you're going to get out of them. Rather than wasting time complaining about your misfortune, use that information to find solutions to your problems.

INVESTING IN THE STOCK MARKET

Now that you've changed your money mindset and created a financial plan, it might be a good idea to start thinking about investing. Many young people still have a bad taste in their mouth about the subject; the stock market crash of 2008 cemented in their heads the idea that investing in stocks was no different than gambling on a slot machine. While it's true there is some risk that comes with any investment, the stock market isn't as volatile as people may like to believe. According to Financhill, people who invested in stocks normally get a return that is better than what they put in about 90% of the time. However, this is only referring to stocks. There are various methods a person can explore if they're thinking about investing, each with its own set of pros and cons.

However, before you even think about entering the stock market, your first course of action should be to create a brokerage account. According to NerdWallet, "A brokerage account is what most investors use to buy and sell securities like stocks, bonds and mutual funds." This is considered your gateway into the stock market, as it allows you to transfer money into and out of your account, letting you reap all the benefits of investing. Only after you create a brokerage account and understand how it functions, should you begin to think about investing.

Stocks And Bonds

Your first thought once you create a brokerage account would probably be to start investing in stocks. After all, that's what the market is named after. However, before you think about investing, it's important that you realize what exactly stocks are. The definition of stocks, according to Investopedia, is "a security that represents the ownership of a fraction of a corporation." Depending on how well the corporation does, the more money you'll earn as an investor.

Stocks are relatively easy to buy and sell; they can be purchased through a broker, and financial advisor, or even online. Their seemingly simple nature is what a lot of people gravitate towards when investing. However, that doesn't mean they're an easy way to get rich. Stock prices can fluctuate quickly and require a lot of research to ensure you don't end up losing all your money. For that reason, you should monitor the stock market frequently, keeping an eye on what businesses are doing well and what businesses are falling behind. This constant worry that your stocks are going to go under also takes a mental toll on some people. It can be distressing to analyze every dip in the curve, every fluctuation price. If you already deal with money anxieties, this might not be the right choice for you.

If you're looking for a little more stability in terms of your investments, then bonds may be a better choice over stocks. Bonds are a loan taken out by a company from the investor. While stocks are very subject to change due to their dependence on the state of the company, stocks fluctuate much less than their more famous counterpart. The downside is bonds on average have smaller returns than stocks and prices tend to fall as the interest rate goes up. People who chose to invest in bonds should expect to have less risk for fewer rewards.

Mutual Funds

Stocks and bonds aren't the only options you have as an investor. There are a variety of different options for you to explore when it comes to investing into the stock market. Maybe you're not too keen on the idea of placing all your money in one place. If you're looking to diversify your investments, then mutual funds are probably right up your alley. According to Fidelity.com, "Mutual funds are investment strategies that allow you to pool your money together with other investors to purchase a collection of stocks, bonds, or other securities that might be difficult to recreate on your own."

Mutual funds are typically composed of about 50 to 200 securities. This effectively spreads your money around rather than putting all your money in one basket. This diversification reduces the risk of you losing a lot of your assets. However, mutual funds don't come without their disadvantages. When you add money to a mutual fund, you do not own any of the stocks within it, meaning you have very little control over where the money goes. Sales charges for mutual funds can also be extremely pricey, with some expense ratios being higher than 1.20% according to Investopedia. It's important for you to analyze all the options on the market to make sure that you aren't overspending on a mutual fund.

Index Funds

Index funds are portfolios comprised of stocks and bonds that match a specific market index. In a way, they are like mutual funds, only their main goal is to align with the current trend of investment results. According to NerdWallet, "Index funds are passively managed and have lower fees than actively managed funds, and often generate higher investment returns."

One of the most common forms of index funds is something called ETFs. ETFs—or exchange trade funds—not only track indexes, but they can also be bought and sold like stocks. This offers a great deal of flexibility for the investor, as well as giving them a more diverse investment to work with. This might seem like the best of both worlds for people: limited risk and greater control over where your money goes. However, like other mutual funds, they are often on the pricier side, as it's often required to pay a broker for their services in setting up the EFT. Your options for diversifying your options may also be more limited. "Investors might be limited to large-cap stocks due to a narrow group of equities in the market index," according to Investopedia.

Each investment—whether it be stocks, bonds, mutual funds, or index funds—has its own set of pros and cons that you need to take into account. By carefully investigating all the options available to you, as well as taking into account your personal financial situation, you'll be able to start investing and earning money in no time.

The act of replacing negative money behaviors with positive money behaviors is no easy task. It will take a lot of time and effort to change the habits that are so ingrained in our psyches. For that reason, it's important that you pace yourself. You don't have to invest in the stock market, put all your personal money into your savings, and develop all your financial goals in the span of one week. It's not a race; rushing your financial success doesn't do you any good in the long run. It has the same effect as doing a 10-kilometer run your first day getting back into exercising. You'll only end up extremely tired and even more unwilling to continue your new routine every day.

By taking your time, you reduce the risk of burnout and it'll be easier for you to continue using these techniques as time goes on. Over time, the actions you take will become more natural as you get into your new routine. By developing positive money habits we're not only bettering our current financial situation, we're also ultimately bettering the quality of life that we'll have in the future.

WHAT IT ALL COMES DOWN TO

We live in a hectic world, and saving or spending money wisely always seems to take a backseat. We all have good intentions when it comes to saving money, but things always come up. We often tell ourselves we will start saving once we reach a certain milestone: like after a certain event, a different season, or maybe the start of a new year. That habit of always pushing our money problems under the rug is one of the reasons so many people find themselves financially insecure. Procrastination will always harm us in the end. We can't wait for our financial situation to get better before we start saving our money. We can't rationalize that we're not in the position right now to start investing. We can't continue to buy needless things, knowing full well that we're going to regret our purchases later. The only way our financial situations are going to get any better is if we make the changes now.

At the end of the day, we are creatures of habit. Our brains are designed to find what works and stick with it. This is one of the reasons why addictions and dependencies are so difficult to overcome. Spending money on things brings us a considerable amount of happiness (even if it is only momentary), while actions like investing or savings give us a considerable amount of stress.

It's easier for us to procrastinate on saving or making better spending habits because those are the things that give us that momentary high of serotonin. Our brains naturally stick with what taps into that "reward system", stubbornly latching on to past tendencies no matter how destructive they may be in the long run. However, luckily for us this often works both ways. The neuroplasticity of the brain makes it so the more we engage in certain activities, the easier it is for us to rewire ourselves and create positive habits. The act of making certain changes sets us up to continue those actions in the long run.

This doesn't simply refer to our habits with money. It also has to do with how we view it, and how we view our current financial situation. People are quick to complain about the misfortune that they have: how the class stratification is unbalanced, how the economy favors certain jobs, how difficult it is for people to pay for college which has only become more important to get good paying work. These are all aspects of life that are out of our control. It's the fault of the people who lead the country, right? Well, this is partly true. There is a sizable amount of injustice that affects people of all races, backgrounds, and classes. However, those factors are a bump in the road, not a roadblock.

As stated by Jaspreet Singh, while the majority are busy complaining about their current situation, the minority are busy finding solutions. When outside factors make it difficult to succeed the normal way, we need to find alternate solutions to our problem. If every person in a wheelchair chose to blame the circumstances that brought them to this point for their inability to play sports, then we would not have established the Paralympics. People with learning disabilities would give up on seeking higher education. People with social disabilities would avoid taking positions of leadership. If we flinched at every unfavorable circumstance, no one would push themselves to achieve their desires. And yet there are people who are naturally put at a disadvantage that are breaking past their shortcomings and achieving the success they deserve every day.

The truth is life isn't fair. People are born into poverty or wealth at random; some people will naturally be in a better place than others. Those are aspects of life that we can't change. However, that doesn't mean our financial situation or our quality of life has to forever be affected by them. At the end of the day, it's all a matter of mind and willpower. The person with dyslexia will often have to work twice as hard to earn their English degree. When outside factors are pushing against us, all we can rely on is ourselves and our own drive to succeed.

Our financial success is based on our own personal desire to achieve it. That drive pushes us to take risks when entering the stock market, to commit to saving our money, and to make the choices with our money that will get us to where we want to be in life. The mindset that we foster over these next few years is what will get through these financial straits.

Money is a necessary evil; it's something we need to be in constant supply of in order to live happy and healthy lives. However, it's our choice what we decided to do with that fact. Will we decry situations outside of our control, or will we work smarter in order to fulfil our financial desires? The first step towards wealth and financial security is the choice to accept ourselves and our financial situation, and to take action to propel ourselves into the future. That's what having a good money mindset is all about.